Hypothetical May Morning

Michael Glover

Acknowledgements are due to the various publications in which some of these poems first appeared: *Encore, Ephemeris, The London Grip, The Tablet, The Irish Review, International Literary Quarterly, Name and Nature: Who Do You Say That I Am?*

Cover image copyright © David Hornung
Cover font copyright © Galdino Otten http://galdinootten.com
Thanks to both.

A number of the poems in this collection were first published in two chapbooks, *Those Lost Days With You* (2011) and *The Quinoa Cake Recipe* (2014)

ISBN 978-0-9935762-9-4

www.1889books.co.uk

For Ruth, ever my blessed armature

CONTENTS

Under The Influence

Those Doggone Bareback Riders

Notes to Harris

Coda

Books

Books

There are books whose thresholds
few would dare to cross.

There are books which spend all day
openly reclining, welcoming
a friendly approach.

There are books which exist solely to play a supportive role
in the lives of other books,
and this makes them light, proud and unencumbered.

There are books which mock, feint and menace
like a fistful of wheedling needles;
and others which threaten bluntly,
straightforwardly – like a quarry hammer.

There are books full of tunnels and twisty,
dark passages where the reader may slip,
slither, stumble or fall.

There are books for high-singing voices,
and others for deep-throats or frogs.

There are books which transform the study
or the public library into a catwalk,
strutting and preening back and forth.

There are sad or unseemly books which hobble,
down-at-heel, and are scarcely able
to spit forth a word.

There are books which scream into our ken –
like a jet into the lives of those camped
beside the runway.

There are books which have been alive for centuries,
and no one – barring perhaps two or three of especial
cobwebby discernment – has even remarked upon
the fact of their being alive.

There are books which exist solely to do good,
and others which stalk abroad with malicious intent
(the first kind may be quickly reduced to pulp
during an untimely spring shower;
the second always know of some place to shelter).

There are books which are fatter than is good for them,
and others so skinny that they are scarcely alive at all.

There are books which love to turn and turn about,
playing games with the reader,
and others which are as straight, dependable and unadorned
as a Roman road.

And everywhere I look there are books to left and right of me,
meting out hope, distress and wild expectation.

The Quinoa Cake Recipe

The Quinoa Cake Recipe
for Sharon

When preparing the ingredients of the poem for the table,
Make sure that each word – and every part of each word –
Is first finely crumbled between the fingers.
Clotted clumps of words make for poor digestion.
Always heat the oven to one thousand degrees minimum.
Cold words are seldom companionable.

Add no word to the mix that you do not yourself understand.
Question closely before admittance all Latin tags,
Semi-conscious Greek heroes,
References to philosophical whimsyings
From the eighteenth or nineteenth centuries.
The ingredients should consist of words
That you know and love
From the neighbourhood store at the junction of
Princess and Division.

Finally, allow to settle for ten minutes at least before serving,
And, first, taste, on the finger's end. Just a smidgen.
Remember: you are not your own poem's most favoured audience.
A fresh-cooked poem is not easily to be judged.
Swelled up poems may later sag,
Poems broad of girth often shrink to a verbal pizzle.
Serve and share while still warm to the gullet.
Take comfort, all, from the drifting aromas.

Already Asleep

Sleepiness is everywhere:
When laws are fresh promulgated,
When the polar bear rears up to kill,
When day skies suddenly darken,
When god steps on this kingdom with his judgemental foot.

It is on such days as these, yes,
That a great tiredness descends.
The newspaper slips from the hand.
The sucked sandwich crust falls from between the teeth.
Sentences, half-uttered, drift away to nothingness.

Oh look, we find ourselves saying, with a careless indifference,
Half-smiling dreamily as we let the glass of bourbon ease
From between the fingers, something is happening at last.
We should go see. After you, my friend...
I nudge you with a foot just then. You are, alas, already sleep.

That Second Cup of Coffee

You are not wholly unlike a kingdom
Risen in its pride from the wastes of the desert:
Golden cupolas gleaming, slow-wavering, musical voices,
Strangers huddled on dusty pavements
Picking their teeth over cards and dice,
The rackety hustle of street markets...

I see it all there, deep inside you,
As you lean to pour me,
With a gentle smile and a single sigh,
A second cup of coffee.

Aerial Surveillance

Kingston is preening its feathers
On the telephone wires above our heads.
Occasionally it smoothly rises, blurry of wing,
And does a quick forward dart
Or a deft double tumble
To a scattering of mild applause.
It says to me (in confidence, surely):
I hold the molten sun in my inner pocket.

Quebec is buying antique collectibles in Market Square,
Making its wishes felt by means of grunts and pointings.
It travels East somewhat later wearing
Loose fitting, vintage English brogues
Beneath a shirt from French Connection.

New Brunswick lives behind the parking lot,
In a makeshift rabbit hutch of sorts,
Staring at a single tree through the wire meshing,
And dreaming of pit stops on the arrow-straight road
To nowhere.
It sings from time to time
Of how the time so easily passes.
It too is not unhappy.

Saskatchewan, unusually, has been squeezed
Between these university houses down on Clergy –
Rain on rusting banjo strings,
Broken rockers on porches,
Doors blaring music.
It is a tight fit during daylight hours.
At midnight anything goes.
Toronto is strutting back and forth on the lake shore,
Eyeing the horizon line and intermittently bellowing.
It plunges in. The water closes over.

The dome of City Hall at its back gleams and gleams.
Macdonald rests in his bed more easily,
The molten sun still warming his inner pocket.

New Age Scene on a Hillside

I have anointed the sheep's carcass for the pyre.
We stand around, open-handed,
Waiting for the manna of fresh-baked bread
To descend, in fisty, crude hewn slices,
From Aurelia's ample wicker basket.

Prayers drift down through the air
In a tongue which feels embracing.
The few clothes we are wearing are far too many.
After all, summer is full upon us,
And we have these deep, supernal urges.

The Overnight Stop

When the light crept under the door that morning,
I remembered, waking, that you had asked me to stay.
I touched the space where you had lain,
The smooth warmth of that hollow,
As you entered, large tray rattling,
Giggling, swearing and still – still! – smoking.

The Cracked Samovar

Some words were nearly spoken today.
Then, quite slowly, you drifted away
Into the next room but one
With your cracked samovar and your broken pen.

Would I have called you Russian
If I had been old enough just then?
Were you a writer, my friend?

I never read a word you ever wrote.
You only ever talked of writing, on and on,
As the days, well, just drifted...
Then you were gone.

Wishing for Canada

Here is all that I would wish for you, Canada:
a sleep of reason in a well-feathered bed
creatures of the wild attending to your every need
ice sheets to ski on, faces tilted up
   to the benignity of the morning sun
coffee at least as good as anyone's

Here is all that I would wish for you, Canada:
good neighbourliness with the bear which prowls
   at your southern flank
poems on street corners, easing the traffic's flow
children to defend you from the dangers
   of a shadowy inheritance
god to embrace you in any way that he knows

Here is all that I would wish for you, Canada:
that your Parliament of Trees will rule wisely
that the Queen's Head will giddily spin for you
that the wildness of the North will never be appeased
that your tongues will bond together in mild-mannered minstrelsy

Why?

I thought for a long, long time about you,
Where you might be right now,
Whose chair your buttocks could be warming,
What mirror you would be looking into.
Not once did you glance back at me.
And so I spoke out loud, almost bellowed, into the darkness.
Are you still hereabouts, my lover, my friend?
The breeze did its usual gentle soughing.
Why am I so – I keep on asking myself – so unappeased?

Bravely Setting Forth in Kingston, Ontario

That mighty prince amongst mannequins,
Once in this thrift-store window,
Has now stepped down into Princess Street
And begun the long walk downtown
To reclaim his destiny.

Neighbours salute him as he goes,
In picture hat, green silk négligée and scarlet hose,
On his way to fresh triumphs
In the churchyard of St Andrew's
(Princess and Clergy)

Where he will lay him down to dream
Of new waves of venturesomeness
Down at the lake shore...
Stepping on board some dainty skiff of sorts,
He will salute Wolfe Island's calm and level strand,

Before bravely setting forth.

On Not Quite Drawing Level

Did I buy you from a thrift store?
Is that why you walk behind me, ploddingly,
When the rain comes on,
Not quite ready to be acknowledged
As my live-in companion?

And yet we sit together in these chairs of an evening,
And you have strong opinions behind closed doors
On what we should watch and why,
And where we should eat and when.
In fact, you would not have me change a thing –
Except not quite draw level
In the open.

The Making of the Quinoa Cake

To be lying, face inclined up to the sun,
Could be a kind of preparation...
For what though, numbskull? Better still
To be frenziedly making in the hot half-light of the kitchen,
Fencing with blurred spatula, fork, spoon,
Playing clashy syncopation with rounded, eight-inch dishes,
Lining it all up for our taste buds' delectation:
Sugar, quinoa, butter, bicarbonate of soda and all the rest,
Mixing and combing and blending, forever blending,
Thrusting it into the deep, hot maw of the ravenous oven...

And then, at last, there you have it, on the table,
In all the rounded warmth of its splendour,
A smooth-topped hillock of sorts,
A landscape to be nibbled at
Once, and then, in memory's deep, blurred glass, forever.
And now I hear it, the clamour...
The odours have drifted elsewhere.
They are queuing around the block,
Down as far as the Wolfe Island Ferry.
They are rapping, with a furious persistence,
On their chipped metal dishes.

The Canadian Mixologist

A short off-cut of pipes-skirling Scottish backbone perhaps,
    finely ground to a thin, oncoming cyclone of eye-blinding dust.
Finger-pinchings of curt English acidities. Add to spice.
Smooth slatherings of French elegance, through-doors-breezing,
    aromatic.
America drizzled in too, clod-booted, brawling a little. Keep a close
watch. Do not admit too easily.

In an English Restaurant

They file in from the close-shaved lawn in tentative ones and twos,
As if for a nerve-jangling game with long established rules
That no one will ever quite lose...
Small, bowed men; taller women, high-coiffured, powerful of step.
Frogs stick in throats and remain there for a while yet.
Once settled in puffed up seats, no words, fewer movements
And even fewer gestures, none rude.
Instead: a slow, gluttonous staring at skilful arrangements
Of modest twistings and shavings of good, rich food.

Slow, reptilian hands slithering
            across the starched white table cloth.
The ache of the manufactured smile, quite quickly switched off.
The sheen of sweat on the brow of the *maître d'*
(salty when, after dark and elsewhere, licked clean off)
Heavily suited on this close summer's evening.
The slow crepitation of nutty bread, quick-finger-broken.

No dog interrupts. No insect. No child. No elf.
The seriously mature have the space all to themselves.
Nothing here roams wild in its restlessness.
One faint murmuration of voices is quickly suppressed.
A single short burst of laughter is deftly plugged
            by a twisted serviette.
Twin glasses rise and chink, and then again,
Until the mind, afloat on nothing, is dreamily at rest.

The courses smoothly pass on by:
Green soups, red radishes,
Jellies at wobble in their own warm amber light.
Spoons, forks, knives are skilfully deployed on time,
And in sequence. Has life every been so much alive?
The evening glides along in such a tame sepulchral quiet.
At the end, all drift away, in ones and twos again,

To lie on twin beds in far-flung rooms
With TV suspended on high,
Tilted, guest-ward, towards the bed, like one of Saturn's moons,
Thinking to themselves: this, surely, is a kind of paradise.

The Ritual

You are wise beyond all reckoning,
Your look seems to say,
As you oscillate gently in your rocker
On this warm summer's day.

You smile at me, wanly.
I am shifting from foot to foot,
A little awkwardly,
With these same glasses, this tray.

The ritual is beginning again,
This ritual which claims us day after day,
This raising of repeated toasts to the triumphs of yesterday
Until, finally, at dark's fall, we almost believe
All that we are nearly saying.

You, here

You are much smaller than I remember.
Perhaps it was not September
When we last met.
The Fall makes for a certain shrinkage of expectation.
Needless to say, I still warm to the idea of you.

But now you are standing in front of me,
With your sloppy bag and your open-mouthed smile,
Asking to be let in for a little while,
Perhaps even for a day or a night or two…
Life, all of a sudden, rushes into
The engulfing darkness of a long railway tunnel,
With a pin prick of light
Ever to be thirsting after…

Advice to an Impassioned Outsider

Attend closely to the following
Or stalk abroad at your peril.
When walking in the street,
Do not shout vulgarities
Directly into your neighbour's face.
Deliver them side-on
Unless he genuinely deserves them.
Good neighbours are to be nurtured
For the good they will do you
When you are down at heel, out of pocket,
Or miles beyond the reach of any hospital.

When exchanging opinions with officers of the law,
Do not assume that your impassioned opinions,
So keen-bladedly delivered,
Are always necessarily the correct ones,
And when he turns to leave,
Do not readily apply a quick forward thrust
Of the foot to the buttock,
No matter how ample or welcoming of
Such treatment it may seem to be.

When driving along the street,
Do not occupy the centre of the carriageway
As if by some time-honoured right.
There are others who may require
Some space, some courtesy.
Gentle the music inside the cab.
Stop thrumming down heavily on the steering wheel.
Hesitate, at least once, before violently expectorating.

Goodbye to Canada

You were here just then, and now you are not.
Who took you away from me?
Did some testy border guard insist
I had no rite of passage?

Depending

The Decision

I ask you to seize this man,
And cause him to suffer all due punishments,
Those of the day and of the night.
It is mete and right it shall be so.
He has stood out against us all these months.

You say he has little clothing.
Such clothing as he has remove from him.
Now plait a circlet of barbed wire,
And drag that length of sacking out,
The one that muffles the wind at the door's foot.

Adorn him with such stuff.
Listen to nothing that he says.
He has said enough, and more than once.
Too many mouths gape when he opens his.
Let his mouth be stopped once and for all.

There is his kingdom, the one that spins in his head,
And then there is ours, of flesh and blood,
Protected by all of you, my precious armoured men.
Now set to. Any hesitation on your part
Could be punished with death. Would you wish to join him?

The Birth

All that needs to be done shall be done.
With the single star standing over,
Solemnity will attend upon the presentation
Of the treasures by the potentates.

Meanwhile, shepherds will blink awake
In the night, and a certain fearsome glory
Will lead them hurryingly down,
Stubbing their bleeding toes as they stumblingly go,

To a cow byre's homely stink, where a bundled child
Will have the fine-wrought shells of its tiny ears
Cocked to multitudes in the God-gracious heavens above,
Which shall be daubed all over with singing.

Jesus is Lord

Imagine a column raised up tall in the desert
Topped by its capital, Doric, Corinthian or Ionic.

See the caravanserai sullenly approaching,
And how the traders whisper amongst themselves
Of its significance
As they make their slow encirclement.

The decision once made,
Watch how the dynamite reduces it
To a heap of dust
Amidst cheers and secret forebodings,

And how, as new morning approaches,
Its long shadow is seen to be returning,
To general consternation.

Observe how they build ramshackle shops against it,
Lean into it, smoking,
And, in time, gently ignore it.

Yes, Jesus surely is Lord.

In the Immediate Aftermath

In the immediate aftermath, the enraged passerby
Removed the cross beam with his own bare hands –
One wrench and it was free. Lifting it on his shoulder,
He hurled it then straight down the hill.
They saw it roll, and hit a rock.

The Man himself was propped against a low wall,
Saying nothing, doing nothing, as good as
Dead to the world. The women were fussing,
Bringing him water, tamping at his wounds with rags.
He paid no attention to this at all.

His eyes were closed, his head slumped forward.
We could see the blood mingled with the greasy hair.
He wanted to say something, but he had no words,
Just a fierce tingling in his hands
From the pressure of all that brute wood and metal.

Carelessly careful

Give no thought to the words that you will use.
The words will choose themselves.
Give no thought to your clothing either.
Your eyes will open, and you will be standing upright
In the chamber, appropriately dressed.

When they accuse you, both look at them
And do not look at them.
There is much beyond their hatred to admire:
The beauty of the desert sands stretching away;
A cup of water raised up in the midst of that desert.

When they enumerate your crimes,
Say over to yourself your ABC,
The one your mother used to sing to you beside the cradle.
She will be there for you, smiling.
And again, when you hang suspended.

She will hold you when they bring you down.
She will wrap you.
You will want for nothing.

A protestation of innocence

I am innocent of the blood of this man.
I have washed my hands cleanly, both sides.
Today my wife is suffering with her dreams.
Take him away, I say. Let him be gone from me.

The blood of the innocent is always bought at a price.
The price is one man dead, and a climate of trepidation.
The ground trembled today beneath my feet.
I want peace in this land. Let him be gone from me.

Someone has thrown silver upon the ground.
They all step around it, warily.
There are ghosts in the street. My citizens run pell mell.
Carry his burden, someone. Let him be gone from me.

Seal his sepulchre with the largest stone.
Do it if you must. It is beyond my reach.
Set a watch over it, night and day.
There was such a darkness today I could not see my hands.

This Man

This man comes along.
He steals the breath from my body.
He scoops the pulsing from my heart.
He leaves me here, in the midst of nowhere.

This man comes along.
He snatches the questions from my mouth.
He wipes the last smile from my face.
He toys with my childish likeness.

This man comes along.
He builds a scaffold for himself.
He climbs up it.
He hangs down from it awkwardly, crying:

Just look at me now, familiar stranger.

The Song of the Easter Canaries

From somewhere hidden behind the back of Easter
There came a sudden and most miraculous
Explosion of joyous canaries,
Each one claiming recognition for its being,
And denying all significance
To the broken, historical Jesus.

Each one carried a tiny wooden
Splinter in its beak,
And with such a splinter
Buildings could be overturned.
Each was ready with a song –
Just four high notes and clear.
No one alive just then
Found that song jarring or wrong.

When the historical Jesus at last woke up
From the death-dream of his crucified misery,
And found himself, damp, in the sepulchre,
In a winding sheet,
It was those canaries who feather-bedded
His difficult repose,

Singing thus to him:
O merciful, broken, miserable one,
We are gathered here to remind you
Of the eloquence of birds.
Have no faith in the trumpets, the organs,
The oboes from on high.
Be quick as we are. Only the quick shall die.

And, once dead, we accept our deaths quite contritely.
We give our feathers to the pillow-slips.
We do not expect to make our individual marks

Upon the consciousness of history.
Be modest, great one, live a smaller life,
Reduce yourself to something
That is more akin to our size...

But did the mighty, historical Jesus heed those words?
Only the stone can tell if he feigned dead,
Only the stone...

The Revelation of Amos

A basket of summer fruit.
And afterwards, death or, at best, despoliation:
Howlings from the rubble,
The crops all failed,
The needy shoeless,
Parading their parched mouths,
And a famine stretching from sea to sea.

And all in the wake of what
The Lord God showed me on that day:
A basket, brimming with summer fruit.

A Word to Theophilus

Theophilus, you will understand why it is
        that I write to you.
It is not in a spirit of levity or frivolity.
It is rather to witness to what I have seen,
And to make it plain to you
That what is rumoured abroad by many
Did indeed happen, and that I was a witness
Amongst those many too.

You have seen my face many times.
It was as true as the presence of my face to you
Is assuredly true.
You have clasped my hand.
What I tell you must be akin
To the clasping of the hand of a trusted brother,
That sure, that firm, that strong.

Do not mistake me in this.
Do not part from me in a hurry
And declare me a madman.
Do not pass me by in the street.
Do not call me a liar.
Leave that to all the others.

Depending

This is the plain, unvarnished truth, Theophilus,
Which we witnessed with our eyes,
Of which I shall write to you in my own hand.
It is trembling, as if to say:
Believe me now, my friend.
You need never believe me again.

He came amongst us, as I shall declare,
Nothing to many, all to some.
He was nothing but a man amongst men.
And yet he was also set apart from us,
As if knowing from whence he came.
The Gadarene swine fled from him,
Plunging down the cliffs.
The very authorities feared him
For the weapon of his tongue.
They plotted. They decided.
They hung him up.
Wresting himself free,
He is amongst us now,
And forever more shall be.

This is all that I must write to you now ...
Dearest of friends, please listen.
So much depends.

Scarifications

Advice on the Flaying of Marsyas

First, to neutralize the mouth
By stuffing the same with compacted sheep's wadding
Well steeped in ram's or goat's urine.

Next, having upended the body,
To bind the ankles with tough twine,
Four times around, until it bites
Into the flesh.
The feet can never be too steadfast.

Having trussed them just so,
Invite six of them to hook the bound ankles
Over the lopped upper limb of a nearby tree
So that the body hangs free, swaying a little –
Push it – having first seen to it
That there is space to pass to and fro
Beneath it.

Let the body be well oiled,
And even slippery to the touch.
That way, the flesh will be easy
To peel back, length by length,
With the aid of a well sharpened knife –
Never use a blade that is blunt.
That could cause torment and delay
To the flayer, whose hourly rate
Is to be borne in mind at all times.

No matter how rapidly they proceed –
And there must be two, at least,
At work at any one time,
Do not expect them to complete the task
In less than six hours flat.
A full-grown satyr is not a child.

Which means that
Given this is a winter's morning,
You must begin at once
And proceed full pelt until the early afternoon.
Not long after that, the light
Will begin to fail
And your precious time will be lost.
You cannot flay by the light of a taper.
It is not the professional way.

So set to work on the dot of eight,
When the sun comes up,
And the victim is freshly awake,
And, momentarily, may even have forgotten
What is in store for him.

Smile at him then.
See through to his innermost being
As the truth of the moment rises through his body
Swifter than the blink of an eye.
Chuck him under the chin with the point of the blade.
Lark about a bit to loosen the muscles of the hand.
Give him a mock-blessing.

In Her Prime

The last to be patient was that concubine,
Flinging the foodstuffs, the plumped cushions,
And still demanding yet more wine
When enough is enough, I had said
As I tossed her back her garter.
I cherished that act
As I cherish all else in this quarter.

Plumped, yes, that's how she was,
Yet she had moved me like no other,
With her pretty, pampering fingers
And that raucous, indomitable laughter,
Pulling at my sleeve so coyly,
Fluttering false lashes...
I knew her name until yesterday.
Then it flowed, ever onward, with the waters.

Much still to be done, oh yes,
The sorting of these papers
As the lackeys gawp on and on,
And I shift my eyes to the pavement
Where they strut and they preen so winningly,
The gorgeous girls of this quarter,
Much like she was when in her prime,
With that small dog yelping after.

Casual People

Casual people striking apples
Down from someone's apple tree...
Someone gave them sticks to strike with,
Someone out of love with me.

Apples, always pendent apples,
Apples hanging from the tree,
That is how I always like them,
Not upon the ground, in heaps.

Someone gave me a red apple
From the tree. She'd struck it down,
A casual person, with an apple,
Staring at me. I stared down.

Apples must be pendent apples.
Apples must not leave the tree.
If the tree one day should drop them,
Strike that tree until it bleeds.

Stepping Aside

Old men must surely step aside,
Giving up the ghost for the future's sake,
Tossing their sticks onto the pyre,

After which they offer up themselves,
Arms twirling before the flames' fury,
Intent on nothing but the numbness of eternity.

Hearing nothing, stumbling awkwardly,
Expectorating wildly into the night,
Nothing but old men in a raging fury,

Wanting, and not wanting, to step aside,
Intent on nothing but the numbness of eternity,
Despising all life – how it stumbles awkwardly,

As it offers itself up to us, stepping, fumbling –
Falling aside into the flames' fury,
Old hurrying men, stick-brandishers,

Hearers of nothing, ghost-bearers,
Thirsters after the wildness of night,
Tossing themselves onto the pyre.

Old men must surely step aside.

Amidst

Amidst the proud, to walk stilt-tall.
Amidst the humble, to corrugate the brow, simperingly.
Amidst the intemperate, to rage oceanically.
Amidst the blandly cheerful, to whistle a hoary tune.

Amidst the gloomy, to sigh full-fathom-five.
Amidst the foolhardy, to toss the second dice.
Amidst the amiable, to extend the open palm.
Amidst the lovelorn, to roll the eye heavenward.

Amidst the hasty, to spring the trap.
Amidst the god-thirsting, to paint the body black.
Amidst the petulant, to iron and crimp each word.
Amidst the despairing, to conjure vaudeville.

Amidst the urban, to bristle the leaf.
Amidst the dead, to clatter the saucepan lids.
Amidst the beatific, to creep spider-like.
Amidst the empty, to be full, fuller, brimming.

Did I Lose You Again?

We were talking together
In that bar in the piazza.
You had asked me for the time,
Lit a cigarette...
I shifted the coffee cups aside,
And, as I was reaching for small change,
I seem to have lost you again.

We were in bed together,
Lying side by side
In that hazy, pleasant drift
Of post-coital contentment,
When the telephone rang,
And I jumped out to answer.
By the time I returned,
I had lost you again.

We were pledged, each to the other.
We had even signed the papers
In that office just off the
Piazza del Popolo.
Do you remember the fussy widow
Who wished us nothing but good?
I felt such joy just then.
Moments later, I had lost you again.

An Exchange of Gifts
for Jesse

She offered me soap on toast
As a breakfast treat,
Purple, lavender-pungent, ovoid in shape.

I offered her nails with crisps
As a snack for lunch,
Silver, hard-headed, and ever so slender.

She offered me brick-in-a-bun
For my teatime taster,
Brown, a mite crumbly, tooth-testing.

I offered her sludge in a bucket
To slake her thirst, daily,
Heavy with promise, slow-moving, marvellously gritty.

Gently Swaying

Down the middle of the street she came walking
With that comely, neat swing of hers,
Seeming both to see me and not to see me,
Being so self-contained in her loveliness.

I felt like some pesky fly to be swatted aside.
And yet I touched my hat, held my stride,
And even walked in step beside her,
Feeling emboldened for the first time in my life.

I told her I knew her name, that it was pretty.
I asked if she knew mine. Not exactly, she replied.
The two of us went on for a little while,
Gently swaying from side to side.

Just then my mother caught my eye,
Burdened down with her baskets,
Picking her way, so slowly, from post office to bakery.
I prayed then that God might translate her to the skies.

Mislaying the Pieces

Somewhere, she said,
I have lost all the pleasures
Of being myself.
I would rather be dead…
He pointed to the shelf:
Po-faced dolls; a frenzy of cuckoo clocks;
That broken-legged porcelain dog…
Was there nothing there to live for?
She thought, defiantly, not.

I have lost, she said,
All the opennesses
Which once distinguished my life:
Mouth, ears, nose, vagina, back passage.
All sewn up by tragedy, diurnal or otherwise.
In which case, he said, how do you
Make yourself heard?
She demonstrated the squeak
Of a nub of chalk
On an old blackboard.

Somewhere, she said,
I have lost all the pieces
Which once constituted a life:
My limbs fling themselves around
Like rubbish in a skip;
My words gush, willy-nilly,
Like water from a faucet;
My eyes swim wildly in my head…
Frankly, I would rather be dead.

He took her loose, thin hand in his just then,
And made some ambiguously worded pledge.

Where Poems Are to be Written

Poems must be written on scraps of used paper,
On the backs of grocery lists,
Instructions to children,
Reminders to renew the car tax
Just before it falls due.

Do not write a poem on a blank sheet of paper
Bought for some special occasion.
A poem is not a special occasion.
It is a thing chanced upon
Which may not deserve to exist at all.
It is accusatory, sullen, rebarbative, meddlesome,
Conversant with soiled linen,
Random droplets of blood, and verbal abuse.

Above all, not being a virgin itself,
It would not recognise the value of purity,
Whether of the white paper variety
Or any other kind.
A poem is a tangled mess of uncertainties.
Pass it by. Try.

Those Lost Days With You

Now that you are closer than you have ever been,
Why would someone take you away from me,
As if to prove that your presence here
Had been an act of impertinence
        on the part of someone unseen?

Now that we are once more here together,
        and our mouths are breath to breath,
Why would a stranger with a book distract me,
Calling me over into the farthest corner,
So that I have to leave you now,
        and attend to what is second best?

Now that you are back from all that travelling
        you surely had to do,
And I have settled your image once again in front of me,
Why are they carrying the tables and the chairs away,
        and even our food?
Is this not after all the day I had been dreaming about,
        the very first of those lost days with you?

The Weight of Nothing

Nothing to take your place but you again
Nothing to be you now you are not you
Nothing to shape itself to something palpable
Nothing to evidence the solid ground

Nothing to ask of something, then to wait
Nothing to be life's substitute – stick, plate, ring
Nothing to threaten, then to smile again
Nothing to be all seasons' partnering

Nothing to be nothing that will ever shape
Nothing to be smallness, bigness, all things in between
Nothing to be that which never seemed to be:
The nothing everywhere enveloping

Somehow

Take it for a moment of inconsequence if you like,
Just the two of us, you and I, together,
Making something of the little we had said,
Feeling a little threadbare, though not quite,
Wondering how much further we would go,
And how many hours before the fall of night.

A moment of inconsequence, yet somewhat special too
Because, once again, we had come together.
No, I had not thought to avoid you,
And you had happened along this same stretch of street
Where we had always walked, of an evening, until recently.
Recently? No, surely not. Much longer ago.
This was hardly the street we had always known.

It was quieter then, with the voice of a single child,
My voice, calling out to yours perhaps,
Though you were not there then, at least not for a while.
I blundered along as I blunder now,
Looking out for familiar things.
You would become familiar too, soonish, somehow.

In Praise of Oracular Speech

Oracular speech quite becomes we spirit-men,
Living here most kindly together,
Gathering in ghosts from farthest corners,
Communing with dust-motes, mouldering mosquito nets.

Oracular speech quite becomes we spirit-men,
Somnolent lodgers in inglenooks or middenward tending,
In daylight hours or as light slow-cedes to darkness,
Our footfalls slow and purposeful, so seldom earth-harming.

Oracular speech quite becomes we spirit-men,
Tongues flashing silver; laughter dark, crepuscular;
Arms windmill-flailing, all worlds encompassing...
Even our close-breathing friends have despaired of us.

Oracular speech quite becomes we spirit-men,
Dust-kissers all, song birds of vanished centuries,
Lovers still blubbering over all that has faded.
Our brightness may yet touch your garment's hem.

Just Being Here

You would fire up the barbecue, you said,
And we could just sit there, and talk, on your new deck,
Built by your own big hands. I'd be holding a can,
Loosely, in my hand, and taking the slow, perfect sip
As the sun, quite lazily, began to dip.
We would talk about your houses, just the two,
And how you missed your seven-acre backyard
Backing on to the park; of how you snarled
When that new-build first appeared –
That first, faint speck of light in the night.
It was another self, presuming, within your line of sight.

You threw up the fences, castellated yourself.
You felt better then, rooted in good earth.
And now you are here, on the outskirts of town.
It all got too much for you. You grew too old.
Now you are close to all the amenities –
Hospitals, penitentiary, morgue –
And a car's quick flight to the mall
To pick up coals for the fire, more cans,
All that life-saving lumber…
Just being here makes you feel a new man.

Queueing at the Cinema whilst musing on the Book of Ecclesiastes

Look neither backwards nor forwards.
Avoid such words as endeavour.
Behind you sorrow looms.
Ahead of you lies disappointment.

Too many have died before you were born.
Too many will die hereafter.
Be steadfast. Close your eyes.
Dream of the footfalls of a stranger.

Stare death full in the face.
There is nothing more certain.
Entertain life as sweetly as it deserves.
Brief will be its enjoyments.

Stare at the plant on the table.
Give it a little water.
Let it cheer you until its petals fall.
Each flower has its moment.

Ask yourself who you are.
Don't expect an answer.
Say to yourself: have I done well?
Pick your own answer.

There is no one left to tell the truth.
The doors are locked. The light is going.
Stand here in this corridor for a little while.
Dream of the footfalls of a stranger.

Only So Many Garlands for the Winter Solstice

Sleep the sweet sleep of the labouring man.
Throw away all you have gathered.
Do not square up to the wind.
You will carry nothing with you.

All go to one place in the end,
Sleeping the sweet sleep of the labouring man.
Clip that shadow from the back of your life.
To be sad is to be better.

There is only so much laughter under the sun.
All go to one place in the end.
Every bone will be shovelled into the pit.
The dead know less than nothing.

The song of fools goes on past daylight.
There is only so much laughter under the sun.
Was not the past better than the present?
Save nothing for your longest journey.

This is a day like any other,
With the song of fools going on past daylight.
When the hands fall idle, the house collapses.
There is no end to the weariness of the flesh.

Conversation is so much chaff on the wind,
This being a day like any other.
He who roots in the earth is gainfully employed.
Dead flies give ointment that stinking savour.

No one can find out the depths of things.
Conversation is so much chaff on the wind.
There is no end to the making of books.
A living dog is no better than a dead lion.

Only so much laughter on the wind.
Only so much crying over spilt milk.
Only so much counting up the losses.
Only so many garlands for the winter solstice.

The Promise

There is no trickery about December.
It comes and it comes, ever overwhelming.
I close the door against it. The door blows open.
I mutter softest greetings. The harsh wind
   hits back at me.

There is no trickery about December.
The key is to be forewarned, to make no bones about it.
You are here in this landscape. It is hell. It is finite.
One foot in front of another. And never forever.

Soon comes the truth of the new year inveigling –
The soft throat of the crocus, the winning blink
   of the snowdrop.
Imagine those beauties, close your eyes
   to disenchantment.
Hot coals may suffice. Spring's promise is speeding.

The History of the Book

Here is that book in which I wrote to you.
The penmanship is so fluid.
There are stains on each leaf –
The measuring out of single tear drops.

Here was that book from which I read to you.
Its pages were so heavy.
Each word was like a drill bit through a tooth.
No wonder I have lost it.

Here is that book which I once gave to you.
You did not accept it.
I found it on the street one day,
Questioning a passing stranger.

Seeing Far

The users of curious arts were prevailed upon then
To pile their books in heaps,
And they were all burned ceremoniously,
Both the books and the men.

I am speaking of necromancers,
Deceitful ones to the core,
Who tore the multitude away
From the light and the truth of the Lord.

There was nothing else to be done.
It was a poison to be drained,
A limb to be lopped,

A mouth to be cleansed of its ill-spoken words.
We are better off without them.
We see now as far as the Kingdom – and even beyond.

The Kite

Patience croons a lullaby.
Cruelty blenches, weeps for its past.
Our book is not alive or dead.
The hours are ever intricate.

Patience croons its lullaby.
Dawn will banish all the ghosts.
Your kiss is only what it was.
The hours are ever intricate.

Patience croons its lullaby.
I set you down. I take you up.
Pages turning in the wind.
The hours are ever intricate.

Patience croons its lullaby.
First I go and then I come.
A kiss is only what it was.
The hours are ever intricate.

Le Cerf Volant

La patience chante une berceuse.
La cruauté blêmit, pleure sur son passé.
Notre livre n'est ni vivant ni mort.
Les heures sont toujours confuses.

La patience chante sa berceuse.
L'aube chassera les fantômes.
Ton baiser n'est que ce qu'il fut.
Les heures sont toujours confuses.

La patience chante sa berceuse.
Je te dépose. Je te reprends.
Pages qui tournent dans le vent.
Les heures sont toujours confuses.

La patience chante sa berceuse.
D'abord je pars et puis je viens.
Un baiser n'est que ce qu'il fut.
Les heures sont toujours confuses.

translated by Robert Melançon

Come Again

I asked you to come again yesterday,
And come you did, though not as yourself.

You appeared as a child at the door,
Sucking its thumb, awkward in its shiftings
From foot to foot. I let you in.

I asked you to come again yesterday,
And come you did, though not as yourself.

You came as a flower carried in by my mother,
Nodding on its stem, so sweetly savoursome.
I touched you then. You sprung to attention
As my mother looked on.

I asked you to come again yesterday,
And come you did, though not as yourself.

You came as a note hastily written in your familiar hand.
I read you from beginning to end,
Such words of encouragement
That we might meet tomorrow.

I asked you to come again yesterday,
And come you did, though not as yourself.

You came as a voice that blows in the air,
Offering me words of condolence,
Words of consolation.
And now I stare at those photographs, one by one.

The Perfect Moment

He looked through the needle's eye
At the city spreading beyond the horizon.
Palls of dust swirled about its minarets.
The calls of the muezzin were sweet to his ear.

Arriving there at evening, he lodged in a local place.
A woman, veiled, young, showed him to his room –
Bare boards, a pot of honey, a pitcher of water,
And a blanket with which to wrap himself against
                              the dust-choked wind.

Rising early, he took in the somnolence of the streets –
A boy bowling a hoop along, a blind man balancing
                              his tray of cigarettes,
Six melons in a row, of which he bought one,
Diced it with his knife, then took each slice, finically,
                              and ate.

The day was looking good.
No one knew who he was.
The guards at the gates of the citadel were nodding.
Yes, this was surely his moment.

The Body Beside the Road

Coming to slowly through the dullest of throbs,
He listened to the debate amongst the people of
How they had doubted his word, and still doubted it,
Of how he was a calumniator amongst men,
Led good women astray, sold trash for more
Than it was worth, walked the streets struttingly
As if he owned them, never once sat still and rested
In the cool of the evening hour, was forever at his
Ear-bending, pouring untruths into the pure hearts
Of children, debating the facts of the universe
With farriers, wood-turners, cattle-men, usurers...

Not once had he stopped until now... Then they looked
Down at him, lying dreamily sprawled there, eyes blinded
By the light, beside that dusty track,
Having fallen into a dead faint at midday
Due to the coruscating heat of the sun.

Thorns and Umbrellas

When our fathers passed beneath a cloud,
Our mothers opened the umbrellas
To save them from all earthly harm.
Our fathers blessed the fabric and the ribbing.

When our fathers passed through the sea,
Our mothers held it apart, like the living room drapes.
They marched triumphal on that day,
Dry of foot, strong of purpose.

When our fathers made the laws,
Our mothers, desk-bound, wrote them down,
Small and neat, from left to right –
The editors, the publishers.

When our fathers were laid to rest,
Our mothers tramped that sacred ground,
Wailing for their bitter loss.
And then the thorns sprung up.

Kerosene in Summer

Not for the second time she saw him arriving
On the smeary yellow Lambretta,
The one that he parked in the doorway.
When he swung his leg over,
She knew it was summer.
Not for the second time,
He chose to ignore her.

She watched him bound up the staircase,
And disappear through the door on the landing.
A squeal for a greeting.
It was night when he came down again
(Two steps at a time),
Though you wouldn't have known that —
Such was the lingering light
Of a late summer's evening.

The smell of hot kerosene
Caught at her nostrils
As she hung in the doorway
After his departure.
She had listened to the dying phut-phut-phut
Of his motor —
A tiny, ridiculous noise,
Worse than any mosquito's.

Dear, Gone Days

Too little luck.
No end of small change.
Promises flung in the direction of futurity.
Dear, gone days.

Passions impounded.
Lickspittles over-ruled.
The majesty of stepping out.
I once stood as tall as you.

When nothing becomes something,
And the books catch fire.
So little for so many mouths.
Entrances ever smaller.

Costly digging, tirelessly.
Trenches make for a groove.
Your tennis days, in a blaze of light.
Less of it, all told.

The Official Reception

The first to leave was the man of moment.
The first to arrive was the man of least significance.
The third to arrive was a woman of beauty.
The fifth to leave was the child with the nose bleed.

The seventh to arrive was the ambassador's uncle.
The ninth to leave was the baby, with its nappy.
The last to arrive was a student, in bewilderment.
The sixth to leave was the man, with a message.

The fastest to speak was the ambassador's wife.
The slowest to speak was the poet, in a suit.
The second to speak was the waiter, offering glasses.
The ninth to speak was the dog beneath the card table.

The first to die was the ambassador himself.
The ninth to die was the shrieking woman.
The second to die was the butler, disbelieving.
The last to die was the man without the invitation.

Forgetfulness

The easiest way is to dispense with all the ritual,
To lay it out on the ground for the flies to feast on,
Not to say a single word over it,
Not even to glance at it on your way to the gaming house.

The easiest way is to dispense with all the fuss and the bother,
To burn all the paperwork, expunge the name from the records.
Memories are short. Life is ever fleeting.
One man does as well as another.

The easiest way is to deny you ever knew him.
I for one have no clear memories of him –
The sighing of a door as it closed, slowly, behind him,
The heckles of a street trader when he ran off with that melon...

The Disappearance

Do not ask what became of you after you left.
You were a nothing, a no one,
The lightest, shortest breath.

Do not ask why we did not pick over your words.
They had vanished
As if they had never been uttered.

Do not ask what name you were given at birth.
The paper was burnt, and the ashes
Carelessly scattered.

Do not ask why your image
Was no longer recorded.
You had no image. We stared through you at the world.

Moaning in Comfort

All told it was a good life,
And so conveniently lived.
After one fell dead, he rose up,
That moment's jack-in-the-box,
Just what the world had ordered.

He looked about. There was a fanfare.
His strutting lasted for more than an hour.
There was astonishment, even pleasure.
Then he packed himself away again.
He knew the distance between here and eternity.

It was a good life, while it lasted.
He was remembered for minutes after.
Then they kicked aside the body,
Straddled it, abused it.
The birds showed precious little curiosity.

The Arrival

Chastisement happens midway through the journey.
We dismount. We kneel.
We expose our flesh.
After the ordeal is over,
We proceed, in single file,
To the gates of the city,
Where we are welcomed as heroes.

Chastisement happens midway through the journey.
We sit in a circle for the ritual of conversation.
Voices rise, insults are hurled,
Physical abuse is not uncommon.
After we are rested,
We proceed to the gates of the city,
Where we are welcomed as saviours.

Chastisement happens midway through the journey.
We close our eyes and listen to the thunder.
Rain lashes our bodies. We rise. We fall.
We renounce our earthly natures.
When the sun rises, we proceed, in some style,
To the gates of the city,
Where we are welcomed as prophets.

Duty

How to be dutiful every day.
To flick the beads of the abacus.
To smile into the face of new morning.
To say hello to the opening door.

How to be dutiful every day.
To fill the bucket at the spring.
To share laughter with friends.
To be guarded in the old man's presence.

How to be dutiful every day.
To cross the road in the traffic lull.
To run where the wind carries you.
To say mother's words after her.

How to be dutiful every day.
To wear black along with the rest.
To sniff deep into the heart of the chrysanthemum.
To walk with a measured pace.

And then comes the sorry aftermath.

Not to Be Seen Again

Not to be seen returning from the garden.

Not to be seen waiting for the housekeeper
To hand over the keys,
With fulsome apologies.

Not to be seen having the last and swiftest
Drink of the evening, and sighing and smiling a little
As you stumble at the foot of the stairs.

Not to be seen thanking one and all for coming,
For the collective gift of their presence,
And for their gifts to boot.

Not to be seen asking which way up
Is the timetable this evening,
And giggling as you blunder into the back of a girl.

Not to be seen fumbling with the ticket at the machine,
Until someone shouts
And wrests it from your hand.

Not to be seen staring at the oncoming train,
And to be dazzled by its lights, its onrush, its clatter.
Not to be seen. And then again. And then again.

Not to be seen forever.

The Remnants

Shred these remnants for rags, dusters.
Give no thought to who might have owned them,
Whose sweat this once was,
Whose arm pushed through this hole.
They are nothing now. Discard them.

Shred these remnants for rags, dusters.
Or, if you prefer it, burn them.
The point is nothing should be left
But a heap of smouldering ashes.
There is to be no sacred remnant.

Shred these remnants for rags, dusters.
Keep out the forensic boys
Sniffing after evidence.
There is no evidence. Whatever happened happened.
The show is over. It's finished.

The Day Before the Auction

I am asking you to be patient with me.
You know my age and my provenance.
You see how I have been treated.
I am not ready to live elsewhere.

I am comfortably settled here,
Partially veiled by this velvet curtain.
The heating could be a little better,
But there is a good view of the skylight.

I am imploring you to be patient with me.
I have lived in this place for as long as I can remember.
Everything has changed around me.
These walls alone are my security.

I am a likeness, though not a good one.
The painter was in too much of a hurry,
Much too much in need of money.
For that I do not hold myself blameworthy.

I say this to you: spare me the humiliation.

Into the Limelight

The deeper the water, the greater the failure of memory.
The keener the blade, the unhappier the victim.
The more sorrowful the stranger, the jauntier the thief.
The brighter the sunlight, the more doleful the shadow-life.

The cheerier the children, the more decrepit the dying.
The more brazen the talker, the more cowed the audience.
The greater the danger, the more reckless the chancer.
The smaller the nightlight, the gloomier the reflections.

The leafier the arbour, the wetter the undergrowth,
The thirstier the runner, the more paradisal the vision.
The keener the grindstone, the more dangerous the sparks.
The beefier the hero, the more shrunken the vanquished.

The more gorgeous the apparel, the more pungent the hedgerows.
The more bountiful the offerings, the thinner the fingers.
The more cherished the beehive, the more golden the glow.
The sooner the arrival, the greater the tragedy.

The Colourist

The colourist in the man gave me this winning look –
Hectic cheeks, a certain brightness of eye.
Otherwise, I would be nothing.

The woman scarcely cared for me at all.
She laid down an outline.
She left the pastels in the drawer, neglected.

Then he stepped up, the lover,
To make me what I am for you now.
He knew you wanted me just so.

He guessed how I could win you.

Hypothetical May Morning

1.

The body has awoken to new beginnings.
You are standing there, on the landing,
Opening your arms to me, and even saying:
Everything we have here is ours, and forever.

The body has awoken to new beginnings.
This house is yours, beside the ocean,
With its open door, still beckoning,
As I stand inside, patiently waiting.

The body has awoken to new beginnings.
We need nothing but this enduring image
Of wood, risen up and perfectly angled,
To make a home for ourselves in three dimensions.

2.

I tell you there is nothing to it.
It is flimsy, slipshod, gimcrack.
Should I continue?
Only a fool would live beside the ocean

In a house such as this one.
What will happen when the winds lift it
Or the sea comes snarling and poking?
Will you be there to defend it

With your pen and your paper, wailing,
Like all good men of writerly pretensions?
Will you expect me to carry you across my back
As you clutch your precious scribblings,

Holding them high as the sea comes surging?
Are you that much of an idiot?

3.
for Jesse

No one must tell you what to do.
Life is still to be invented.
Take this bird, for example.
Who invited her here?

Life, with its bygone pleasantries,
Its rearing ladder, its bird-feeder,
Is opening out to us again
On this morning least expected,

A hypothetical May morning,
Wedged carefully in
Before the promises of summer.
Seize it now. Grasp its fleeting blandishments.

Under the Influence
i.m. John Cassavetes

Under the Influence

I catch you back from all that falling
When you are at your least forgiving.
You look through me.
You set me aside on the end of the table.

I call you, repeatedly, for an explanation.
You sound perfectly normal.
You let your shoes do the walking. Pretty.
You raise the hemlines of your dresses.

No matter how much I shout, you still do not notice.
I am a shrunken pea in your company.
You walk over me when you notice me at all.
You dribble and you sing, airily, in the bedroom.

You Interrupt Me

I never wanted you back here.
I wanted you to remain as you were, far distant from me.
I wanted the luxury of contemplation
Without the daily complications.

Yet still you come banging at this door, pleading.
You are drinking too much again.
                        Your smiles are too loose-weave.
Why not gather up the men around this table,
And stuff them all into your pocket?

I can barely breathe beside you.
I feel crudely myself, ape-like, grovelling.
I call to you from somewhere far above me.
You fall on my head, clunk, like a meteorite.

Your Childish Ways

You play around with the children
Because you are a child yourself.
You join in their games of make-believe.
You are the first with the costumes.

You cork-blacken your upper lip. Ridiculous.
You attach purple wings to your shoulders.
You dance, all of you, in front of me
As if life is not allowed to be SERIOUS.

I need to knock you into shape again.
I need to strip you bare of all this nonsense.
One day you were born. Remember?
Then one day you grew up. Forgotten?

Keep Away, Mister

That burst water main kept me from you.
So you stepped out into the street, hips rolling,
Singing to yourself as you drank in the billboard music.
They had to clear a space just to watch you.

He was ready for you, being at a loose end.
He ordered. He couldn't get to the bottom of your thirst.
When he carried you back, he was in for the kill –
Or so he was thinking, that no-hoper.

He ran out on you, he was that frightened.
I could have told him. I could have warned him.
Keep away from that woman, I would have said.
A thousand volts are forking through her body.

Starting Over

The doctor had no choice but to commit you.
None of us could control you.
We were at the end of the road. There was no future.
What is a future without a future?

What my mother said was out of line.
You weren't wacko. You were never wacko.
You were looking for something somewhere.
Nobody knew how to look with you.

And now you are back, showing some patience.
There's a lid on you. Your mouth is zipped.
I think we should send all these people away.
We need to start our married lives over again.

Sucked up to Paradise

I have no authority to give you.
I have no authority myself.
I am a raging bull of a man.
I pulverize everything I look at.

I want you to clear some space for sweetness.
Everything in here is jagged or broken.
I look at you askance sometimes,
Scarcely believing what I'm seeing.

There's such beauty in you. Always has been.
Your hands flutter so delicately.
When you lay down a smile for me,
You bear me up to paradise, Mabel.

Nursing Confusion

My hand descended upon you like the hand of a stranger.
I don't know how it happened.
I want to tear myself limb from limb.
You are too precious even to be touched.

And yet I touched you.
I made ugly marks on your body.
I kiss all those places now, one by one.
My hand was a brute's hand, a stranger's.

I am kissing you now as we lie together,
Staring out into the garden where the children are playing.
Soon enough you will run out there like a child yourself,
And I shall be lying here still, nursing my confusions.

The Final Credits

The end of the world comes, too soon, too quickly.
And you are not with me.
You had said your goodbyes long ago,
And I had grown into a different man altogether,

More regulated perhaps, niftier on my toes,
More inclined to seize the opportunities presented.
That was not the child-of-a-man you married,
That was not the boy who took a bath with you.

And now the end of the world is here,
                                        too soon, too quickly.
I don't know where it is that I'm going.
I snatch at passing hands. I smile into faces.
None of them is your face, Mabel.

Hurrying

I had begun to write this note to you.
And then, without reason, I stopped again.
I had it in my head, all the words I wanted to say.
I was laying them down in a very particular order.

And then I heard birdsong just beyond the window.
I stood up, and lit myself another cigarette.
I needed to stretch myself.
        I needed to listen out for the music.
Birdsong was so rare in this neighbourhood.

When I sat down again, your face had shifted.
You were no longer looking towards me, enquiring,
Lips parted, in that way you used to do.
You had stepped out somewhere.
        You were already hurrying away.

Guzzling

Goodbye, Mabel. I never thought I'd say those words.
Goodbye, Mabel. I never thought
                    I'd hear myself saying them.
You were always my most cherished wish.
That is why you left me, because I burned for you.

Burning is dangerous, two people on fire,
No dousing of the flames, no rescue.
Two heaps of charred ash, mute, inglorious,
That's what we became eventually.

I am not that, you said the words yourself.
You Phoenix you, you slipped into the nearest bar
And ordered the tallest drink on offer.
I still laugh to see you there, head thrown back,
                    guzzling like a pig.

Our June

June was so lavish that year.
Beers out on the porch. All that drunken laughter.
I didn't get my hands dirty once.
I left my boots outside, unloved, unwanted.

June was so pretty – like a child that jumps up
                              and kisses you,
Almost knocking you over.
We sat beside one another on those tubular chairs.
That was as much as we ever needed.

June was so special that year,
Unlike any other June on record.
I'd keep it in this jar if I could,
Lid screwed tight, out here on this window ledge.

Laughter

You say we're laughing all the time,
But there's no laughter in the laughter.
It's all just a kind of crazy blurting out.
It makes no sense. It doesn't add up.

I hate your jokes. They're always stupid.
They're better not spoken at all.
You roll your head around when you say them
As if you've lost control of yourself.

So: no more jokes and no more laughter.
Let's be solemn for a change, let's be serious.
There's a lot of shadow in this life.
Let's lie back on this bed and just stare at it.

The Crucifix

There's no God in any of this.
I don't know why you hung that crucifix.
It's a great ugly thing above the bed.
I never wanted it there. Sell it.

It could be melted down, a piece like that.
We'd get good money for it. We could convert it
Into beer, food, even a new truck.
That truck out there looks so woebegone.

Or you could give it back to your mother, damn her eyes.
She could do with a crucifix hung from her fat neck.
I don't want her around here again today.
I may even bop her with the thing – like this, baby.

Youness

I love the way you are so light on your feet.
I love your cat-like smile too.
Someone must have gifted you with these things,
Someone mysterious, who really cared for me.

I hardly hear you when you approach me –
From behind is best, with a nibble at my ear.
Then I catch at your hand and lead you around
Until the miracle of you stands in front of me:

All of you, all that there ever was,
As much as I can take – and more,
Overbrimming with yourself, nothing but youness…
Even if you took yourself away, I'd never give you back.

Pointless

Everything we say could have been said by someone else.
It's that trivial, that pointless.
Why can't we cleanse our mouths for a change?
Are we both too stupid?

I don't even listen to most of the words.
I just see your mouth opening, showing your teeth,
Those beautiful teeth of yours.
I want those teeth. They are my most precious objects.

That's strange though, isn't it? Good teeth. Bad words.
We vomit up the stuff like a street sewer.
How much do I care about any of this?
What do I remember when I close my eyes?

Forgetfulness

I had clean forgotten the woman,
That whore with the diaphanous veils
Who went about the city, harp in hand,
Making sweet melodies.

I had clean forgotten how I followed her
Into that maze of alleys behind the fish stall
Where she would sing her small lamentations
Over the loss of all that she had known –

Her presence at the old Theatre Royal,
Playing every *grande dame* known to mankind,
She had done it all in her time.
And now she was trapped behind the fish stall,

Playing to my appetite alone.

Those Doggone Bareback Riders

Those Doggone Bareback Riders

Groping in the dark for the knob of the door,
He burst into a street of loutish bare-back riders
Thundering back and forth, and caterwauling
Through their desperate, endless seeking out
Of that late morning's rodeo.
But was he equipped to make his mark,
Feeling, as he did, so lonely that day and so set apart?

Feeling, as he did, so lonely that day and so set apart,
He peered through the lens at all those microscopic particles,
Untold numbers of them, zigging and zagging around,
And wondered about envying their energy,
Their sheer addiction to the joyousness of life
Even while they were pent in a chamber so doggone confining.
Could he be such another? The spurs glinted. Sighing, he mounted.

Was I Not?

Was I not here when you called?
There must have been some mistake.
I had settled myself in a chair
With a drink. I was fully awake.

Was I not here when you called?
Do I not remember your voice?
There were other voices, on other days,
All quite seductive, of course.

Was I not here when you called?
Did we not kiss and then speak,
Clasp hands, make a joke,
Say how little we'd changed?

The Good Neighbourliness of the Dead

The dead sleep with you.
They listen to your thinking.
They speak the words that you utter.
They walk in step with you to the market.

The dead console you when you grieve.
They invite you to stare into their faces.
They prepare a bed for you to lie on
When your limbs prove insupportable.

The dead sing with you –
High notes, pure notes, unending.
When you close your mouth, listen.
The singing is ongoing.

The dead are your best of friends.
They have gone before you.
They have swept the path until it shines, clean and bright.
They have cleared away all the debris.

Do not despise them.

The Gift

I was with you again just now.
Tell me what I told you.
I held your hand as you were leaving.
I waved goodbye to you on the threshold.

I said to you: remember not to forget.
You looked past me, still dusting.
When you pulled on your shoes, the red ones,
I caused you to hesitate, in the bedroom.

I was with you again just now.
I saw my clothes again, still hanging in the wardrobe.
I reached out for my familiar jacket,
Plumped out at the shoulders.

I was with you again just now.
Holding your hand as you were leaving.
I said: the stream bed still thirsts for water.
You looked at me then. You seemed to remember.

Perfect Peace

No one lives here.
No one listens.
No one takes stock.
No one remembers.

No one counts the stones in the wall.
No one hurriedly washes.
No one paces back and forth.
No one tends all these graves.

No one sighs.
No one raises a voice.
No one faces into the freezing wind.
No one howls in the teeth of the adversary.

Yes, it is all perfectly peaceful now.

Those Hard, Necessary Words

If a son should accuse me of betrayal,
I would tell him straight off: I am not your father.
If a daughter reminds me that I have failed
To provide her with stockings, shoes and various cosmetics,
I drag her to the balcony overlooking the street,
And say to her: just look you down there
At the beggars meekly extending their wizened fists
For coppers or even a mouthful of half-chewed gristle.
If you wish to join them, be my guest.
Unless you should choose to remain here,
Prinked and pampered like all the rest...
At that, the gaggle of servants at my back
Who have tiptoed up to see what there is to be seen,
Re-sheathe their daggers, and return to the gentle dusting
Of objects of immemorial splendour and importance.

One Yellow Glove

I leave you as I found you,
Filling a space in the doorway,
With the questions unanswered:
Who you were,
What you'd come for exactly,
Why, soon, you'd be leaving.

I leave you as I found you,
Awkward, shy, improbable,
Green hat at an angle,
A coat that hung off you,
And one glove,
Which is why you had come here,
You told me,

Filling the space in the doorway,
Enquiring if I'd seen it,
              Another like this one, yellow,
And patterned.
I looked at it.
I looked at you, looking,
And I wondered…
No, we never found it.

From the Couch in the Kitchen

You are a master of docility,
Measuring with your eye
The fly's slow creep
Up the dank kitchen wall.
Occasionally you may shift a saucer
If it presumes to block
A new resting place for your wrist.

The pen has not been picked up
Since a week last Tuesday
When a note to your sister was written.
Unposted it still sits, beside the cup
Half full of cold tea
From which, from time to time,
You still sip.

You think of her bulk at your door,
So bright-shining, in her over-sized dentures,
Gob full of blather.
Then, with the briefest of brief sighs,
You make as if to turn over.

No Words

It was night when you found me,
On the ground, between the bushes,
Sprawled, slack-limbed, as if in sleep.
You nudged me with the toe of your boot.

On any other day, I would have woken,
And, seeing you there, smiled up at you,
Stirred a little, yawned, disbelieving,
And accompanied you to our favourite places.

Not on that day. I was sullen, unbudging,
Hearing nothing of what you said to me,
Feeling nothing when they heaved the weight of me,
Having no words to deny your misery.

Cold as Charity

Establish today this makeshift garden,
With its juniper tree here, its rose arbor there.
Marie Berthot has been invited to sit in it,
Wisely cradling her ancient secateurs.

When the breeze wafts in, you rise
And talk to the gardeners who are just now arriving
In ones and twos, greener than any greenwood tree.
How harmonious it all seems.

At the end of the day, the demolition work begins.
You listen to the felling of trees
From your bed at the back of the folly.
How cold the nights are these days!

Colder than charity, someone said.
Charity is the maid who attends upon you these days,
Bringing a glass to slake your thirst,
Your much prized gardening manual to sleep with.

You Were Always There
for Ruth

You were always there,
Deep in the darkest plunge,
Beneath the cowering light,
Above the highest cloud,
Under the dampest shower.

You were always there,
Between the meanest words,
Across the widest space,
Within these shadowlands,
Beside the youngest oak.

You were always there,
Inside the tightest box,
Within this tender leaf,
Beyond this dizzying world,
Making your way to me.

Notes to Harris

1. The Dog-Days of Summer

Bleary-eyed from sleeplessness,
And a little ragged at the edges,
We are waiting in vain
For the coolness of evening,
The sweet amiability of Fall weather.
Summer has been too much with us.
Legs drag, in dutiful pairs, across the street.
Even the milk carton has put on weight.
Where do we go to in these days?

Nowhere in particular.
We slink around the parking lot,
Blistering finger tips at the touch of the bonnet.
Should we siphon off the gas,
And bury it in a hole in the cellar?
That would be dangerous, we are told.
That would be to encourage a great *whoomf* –
And yet more heat.
To die, so untidily, would be a losing game surely, Harris.

2. Where are you, Harris?

We say so little to each other these days, Harris.
The conversation does not ebb and flow
Between cool sips of beer
As it once used to do.
Are we unlearning each other?

I look again, deep into your pock-marked skin.
You are someone else. Or so it seems.
Perhaps there is a look of elsewhere in your eyes.
Perhaps you are seeing some woman idling
Down a side street unknown to me.

3. In the Boat with Harris

After the outboard had sputtered for a little while,
The boat bucked forward onto the water.
It was so cool this morning,
The trees so shadily enveloping.
This is how I like my Canadian Shield,
I was thinking to myself as I bit down upon
A second cream doughnut for breakfast.

You were barely steering at all,
But nothing seemed to matter.
Neither of us knew where we were going.
There was nowhere to be going today.
To be together on this lake
Was to be everywhere and nowhere.
It felt a little like a small child at prayer.

4. Asking Harris a Question

Is your name boring to me today, Harris?
Or is it that I am too much used to it?
I kick it around when I say it
Like a rusted can in the street.
And yet, after a while I go to pick it up
And place it on the wall next to the garage.
I wouldn't want an old car to roll on by and crush it.

Does my name feel the same way to you, Harris?
You have never told me.
You use it as often as I use yours.
But do you say it warmly?
Harris, I say out loud, hoping to hear my name again
To test your strength of feeling.
Shut up slob, I'm still sleeping, you reply, turning over.

The tent nearly goes over.

5. Harris Tweed

I read it once: Harris Tweed.
It made me laugh just to think of it.
When I see him next, I tell him.
Did you know you were tweedy, Harris? I say,
Pinching his jacket. He's pissed off.
So what's with you today? he grunts, shrugging me off,
What's with the English stuff?
We walk towards the mall together, in silence.
There's the entire week's allowance to spend
And our friendship to consider.

6. Going Nowhere in Particular

I took you nowhere in particular I had been before.
It wasn't that kind of a day.
Where are we going? you said
When I took a quick turn left.
To the races, I replied, stiffly.
Then we waited, on the edge of the park,
Watching the kids doing wheelies.
One of them fell off and cried.
We dusted him off.
Had enough? I said.
Harris just stared at me.
He had that lost, hungry look in his eyes.
It's the Ritz then, I said.
We both solemnly agreed.

7. Two Step

When Harris comes by,
It all starts again,
Those trickles of conversation,
The slow, slouching walk,
The way even our shadows seem to fit.

Neither of us has said anything about all of this.
It wouldn't be right.
Even our coat collars get turned up, in sync,
On these cooler nights.

8. The Glow

Did your mother say that you could?
I didn't ask her, he replied.
The watch looked loose on his wrist.
It swivelled when he shook it.
Don't lose it then.
He scowled at me, jerked down on his sleeve.
I could still see the glow through the shirt.

9. Rivals

When did you get taller than me?
It's bananas, he said,
As we squared up back to back.
I could feel the heat of him, pressing back.
Don't ease up on your toes.
I'm not, he snapped.
It's the slope of the road.

10. The Dream

I had a dream of you beside me.
What was I doing?
Just the usual nothings –
Picking your teeth,
Shifting from foot to foot.
It's just great, he grinned,
How neither of us ever changes.

11. The Balloon

Once I had a dream about you, Harris.
You were a big boy, bigger than me,
Bigger even than the world
You dandled in your hands,
Left to right, right to left.
I just stared at you then.
You were so awesome
Until this arrow came winging,
And the world deflated.
You deflated too.
You were small enough, by the end,
To be standing, looking up at me,
On the end of this shoe.

12. The Big Shrug

I've never known a kid like you, I tell him,
Never listening to what other people say.
What did you say anyway? he says,
Spitting out the words.
It wouldn't matter now. The moment's passed.
What moment? he says, long-faced.

I never saw any moment breeze by.
That's because you were asleep when it happened.
And, by the way, I wish you wouldn't shrug your shoulders
In that stupid way.

13. Coffee

They're dredging the weed from the pond,
And we are just looking on,
Wondering what kind of a day it is,
With the clouds all built up overhead.
It's colder than it was, I say.
Harris says he's not cold at all.
You're so weak, he adds, flexing his arm.
Then he picks up this rock and smirks at me
Until the weed man turns round, and he puts it down.
We're both thinking coffee just then.
What a pair of sad clowns, the man says, as we walk away.
He doesn't even hear the filth from our mouths.
Only a deadbeat gets to dredge a pond.

14. Cans

When did we first start off drinking coffee all day?
He gives me this sigh for an answer,
So long and so lonely,
Then stares down into yet another empty cup.
Is it the sixth today?
We're both feeling good by now.
We walk fast.
We talk fast.
We throw these cans into the graveyard,
One by one by one. It's fun.
Walking back that way at eight,

The man who digs the graves hands them back,
A whole black sackful.
Do something with these, he deep breathes,
Jangling them at our feet.
By then the coffee buzz has worn off.

15. Gone Out

Harris has gone out for the day,
His mother says, flicking her ash downwind.
Where though? He never goes out.
There's never anywhere for him to go.
I tell her that. I tell her straight.
He's a new kid these days, she says.
You should learn from him a little bit.
You're not good for each other, you know.

Where have you been? I say,
When he walks up, just moments later.
Nowhere, he says. Where's to go?
I just look at her then.
I stare hard into her vacant face
Before she lights up again,
And then blows out some more smoke.

16. Saying it Again

I wish I wasn't so sick of Harris and his face.
He always says the same things all day.
I could say them for him if he asked me.
You know, he says, looking up at me from his coffee,
I'm just sick of you and your habits.
Why can't you be like someone else for a change?
I know every word you're going to say before you say it.

Touché. Touché.

17. The Ring

Harris deals the cards out one by one.
You're so slow, I say,
Hitting the table with my fist.
Why don't you speed up?
There's more fun in the game like that.
I like dealing slow, he says,
Eyeing me from under his cap,
Which is pulled down low.
That's how they always do it, the good ones.
Its all part of the finesse…
There's a ring of coffee on his upper lip.
He doesn't know that yet.

18. Old Folks

I just wish things weren't as they are, I'm explaining to Harris.
How do you want them to be then? he says, reedily.
We have money. We have hope.
What hope? I reply.
He jangles the small change in his pocket.
We both look down the street just then
At the old folks coming on,
Swaying towards us.

19. Gum

I got him some gum on his birthday.
It could at least have been the whole packet!
You're so ungrateful, I tell him.

You just suck.
I thought of you, didn't I?
Ok....
He hands one over.
That's more like it.
What's friendship about if not sharing?

20. Bad Tuesday

Tuesday was really, really bad.
Tuesday was when nothing happened.
Harris had lost what little we had
Of the allowance.
Let's keep on looking, I say,
Staring up the street.
But we've looked everywhere already, he says.
We sit outside the coffee shop all morning,
Watching them drinking our money,
Feeling angry and sad,
Really more angry than sad.

21. Flies

I'm getting this job tomorrow, I told him.
What job? he says, lower lip curling.
That job in the car shop.
I thumbed in its direction.
I just love staring at flies, Harris says.
He'd been barely listening.
He never listened
When you talked about the future.
The way they crawl up walls, he droned on,
The way they walk upside down on ceilings...
Flies are just magic.

22. The Empty Lot

Have you seen all this space?
We've stopped outside a vacant lot on Main Street.
Isn't this new?
Where did all those buildings go to, Harris?
I feel upset.
The dust is choking my throat.
I loved that car shop, I tell him.
I kicked balls against that wall, plenty...
Take it easy, he says, rubbing my back.
He nods like a cute toy dog behind a windshield.
There'll be something else there soon.
But not the same things, I tell him.
I love the same things to be there, forever!
You have to move on, friend, Harris says, soothing.
The future's all clean and new.
Don't spoil it!

23. Finger Jiggling

What's wrong with your hand?
Nothing. I'm just practising.
He jiggles his fingers again.
Then he goes as if to throw something.
Except that there's nothing.
I'm practising. He says it again.
For what though? You can't practise for nothing.
I haven't decided just yet, he says.
There are so many possibilities.
Life feels so open...
I wish I could have wiped the stupid look off his face
When he said that just then.

24. Going Nowhere

Where are we going today, Harris?
Where are *you* going? he corrects me.
I'm staying here.
Nowhere is my final destination.
Why not go somewhere though? I say.
Because life's just too rich inside me, he replies,
Settling into himself on the wall
With a large cherry coke beside him.
So I just get up, walk away,
And wait for him round the corner.
I reckon three minutes.
Not quite that long, as it happens.

25. College Stuff

Harris pushes me off.
I'm sleeping! he says.
But you only just woke up.
You can't sleep all day.
I think when I sleep.
I'm thinking now.
About what?
He opens one eye.
In colours, not words.
You wouldn't understand about that.
Colours as symbols...
For what?
Life, death, all that sort of...
College stuff.
You wouldn't know about that now, would you?

26. The Cheeseburger

Why did you walk out before the end?
Because I knew the kid would die.
It was just so boring.
He was sitting on the wall, eating.
You see, he had to die.
It was the only way forward.
He'd kept my cheeseburger warm in his pocket.

27. Playing Stupid

Sometimes Harris just grins for no reason.
He even snorts down his nostrils like a train or something.
What's the big joke? I ask him.
You wouldn't understand.
That really maddens me.
So one day I do the same.
I think about nothing. I grin.
I even slap my knees.
He just ignores me.
It's as if nothing ever happened.
Why didn't you even ask me?
I say to him later.
Ask what? he says.
Why I was doing all that!
He just looks at me
Like I'm something shiny and plastic from China.
I didn't even notice. Reason?
You're always playing stupid.

28. Midnight Child

How old are you now, exactly, Harris?

I'd been wondering again.
You mean to the last second?
No, stupid!
Why do you want to know?
Well, you think you're older,
But I'm not so sure any more...
I'm a child of the morning, he says,
Snapping his fingers,
Fresh-faced, eager to be alive –
Unlike some other people...
Sometimes he really needles me.
My mother did say it once though.
It was midnight when she had me.
She was plain exhausted.

29. The Fastest Train

Out of the blue he just says it:
What would be the fastest train to nowhere?
He nudges me. I keep on reading the funnies.
Could you name it? And if you could, would you catch it?
Next he pushes this stick in front of my nose.
Could you jump over this? he says.
I set my reading aside.
Why are you being so boring today, Harris?
I don't exactly know, he replies, sighing.
Sometimes I just wish I was someone else.
Who then? I'm getting interested now.
He scratches his chin. Points two fingers at my two eyes.
Anyone in this world but you, buddy.

30. Evil Ways

Did you ever want to kill somebody? I ask him.

We're leaning over the bridge, just sniffing the wind.
The traffic's rip-roaring beneath us.
I could maybe do a drone kind of thing, he says,
Like dropping a brick from here, and then running away...
But then I'd never be sure I got him.
We don't talk much after that.
I just keep on looking at him, though not directly.
The walk back to the mall feels a long one.

31. Just Walking

Are you walking the same way as me? he says, stopping.
We both stop together.
Would I do that! You must be crazy.
We both stare down at each other's legs.
Let's start over then, he says, and just see...
I'm not moving! I tell him.
I'm not pretending I'm you.
Would I do such a thing?
So who's going to change then if it's true?
We're still wondering.

32. Brain Death

Do you like it here? Harris says, breaking the silence.
We're both staring down at the mill pond.
Not bad. Better than most places.
Did you ever see a fish in this water?
Ugh. Ugh...
They're all dead. That's why.
Then, raising his head to the sky, he says:
Too much toxicity in this region...
Why aren't *we* dead then, Harris?
He sticks his toe in the water, dragging it sideways.

Brain death's a slow thing for sure.
Didn't you notice how I'm slurring my words?
That's not some kind of a fashion statement.
We leave soon after.

33. Toxic Waste

Don't you just love trains, Harris says,
All that whoo-oo-ooing?
It's so haunting.
One goes by just then.
The ground shudders.
I count how many sealed carriages.
What's in 'em, do you think?
All toxic waste, Harris says,
Headed off for China.
The quicker it gets there the better.

34. Not Leaving

When are you leaving exactly? I ask Harris.
He's examining a rock he's just picked up.
That guy's always looking.
I'm not going he says, shrugging.
You're not going! Why though?
Too expensive.
My dad just got laid off.
Too bad, I tell him.
I don't need all that college stuff, he tells me.
Anybody with a mind can think.
True enough.

35. Snails in Hiding

This town is getting way too expensive.
One cherry coke between us
To last the whole of Thursday!
We're walking everywhere,
Seeing things we never even saw.
I never knew how many snails
Lived behind billboards.

36. Dear Harris,

I'm going away for a day or two.
Don't try to reach me.
Don't take it personally either.
That would be stupid.
I just need some space in my life.
Sometimes I feel I can't even breathe.

We meet a bit later.
Where did you go to? he asks me.
Wherever I needed, I reply.
Just don't hassle me.

Why does Harris have this way
Of getting up my nose?

37. Muttering

You talk too fast, I tell him.
Your words are a blur.
You never make sense to me,
Even when I can hear you.
He walks away then,

To a different bench altogether.
I watch him. His head's turned away now.
He's muttering into the wind.
You don't have to pretend to be talking!

38. Stupid Weather

Who made this stupid weather?
I can feel how it's flattening my hair.
God, Harris says,
Friend to the lonesome...
I think about that
As I'm watching them hurry,
In twos and threes,
Up the sidewalk.
Take it easy, lady!
One of them nearly goes over.
Is God into practical jokes?

39. Being Marty

Why don't we go somewhere today, Harris?
We are somewhere, he says. We're here.
But we're always here!
No we're not, he says,
Switching on that clever clever grin of his
Like I'm the one that's being stupid.
Here is always different. Didn't you ever notice?

I'm staring at Marty's just over the road.
He's sweeping the street
Like he's always does,
Slowly, slowly, half bent over,
Then picking up the cans

In his finicky twisted fingers.

Harris, I tell him,
You are so clever that you make me sick.
He snorts down his nose.
He has this maddening way of shrugging me off.
The only way is to pretend not to notice.
So I shout over:
Hi, Marty, hi big fella!
And Marty, being Marty, salutes me.

40. Silence

Sometimes I just don't know
What to say to you, Harris.
Don't talk then, he says,
Just listen to the silence.
We're on the edge of the wood,
Facing out, just sitting.
There's not too much traffic,
It being a Monday.
So I close my mouth.
Should I close my eyes too?

How long was I asleep for?
I'm asking myself
As I walk back behind him.
That's another whole day then.

41. Old

When is old really old, Harris?
I'm watching this old man,
Shuffling along,

Just not seeing us.
Is your brother old yet?
No way, José! he says,
Swinging his big face round.
He's into basketball.
He jumps as high as the net, higher...

I try to imagine that,
With the size of his belly.
How old is he then?
Harris thinks a bit
As he bites down on his lip.
Forty-two maybe...
And how old is old then?
We're both thinking: 60, 90, 80...
Those numbers just keep on
Up-and-down racing
Like we're throwing balls into a net,
Balls we're not catching
When they fall back.

42. Bad Tooth Day

Harris is having a tooth fixed today, he tells me,
Pointing, and half-opening his mouth.
He bit down on something,
A rock or something.
He doesn't really want to talk about it.
He makes this gesture of zipping up his mouth.

I've never known life to be so quiet.
When we walk side by side on the sidewalk
I'm staring down at our feet
Like they're something interesting to be seen.
I don't even know what to think about.

I tell him I'm not feeling too good either,
So we say our goodbyes to each other.
I watch him slouch away, hands in pockets.
It's the worst of our days together, I'm thinking.
If I was my sister right now,
I swear to God I'd be crying.

43. Crocodiles

I'm looking at Harris, thinking:
He's bigger today. Something happened.
And so I say it. I stand next to him, looking up,
And I say: what's with the heels, Harris?
He looks down at his shoes, embarrassed.
They're black, and long at the front,
Like they got an extension.
These are my crocodiles, he says,
Twisting them in the air.
She bought them at the mall.
I wasn't even with her.

44. Ice Cream Day

Are you sick of just being yourself? I ask Harris.
It's ice cream day.
The heat's beating down on us.
He closes one eye.
Nope, he replies, after a while.
Why though?
Because there's always someone else to be
If you think carefully about it.
It's a question of how many locks and how many keys…
I think about them all,
Ranged side by side on a shelf
In some lonely garage I never even noticed.

Then I take the next lick, slowly,
Scooping it all up.

45 Squeeze Me

He's wearing this badge on his jacket.
Red like a fat tomato.
It says SQUEEZE ME.
He's just staring at me staring back.
He's biting down on his lip,
And I'm bent over, killing myself,
Looking up, pointing, and then
Killing myself all over again.
Stop! he says. Stop!
But why would you do such a thing? I'm saying.
I just don't believe it.
She *made* me do it, he says.
She said she wouldn't see me again
If I didn't wear it.
It was her special gift.
All the time though? Are you crazy?
He rips it off.
This means we're finished.
So – no big deal – we're finished.

46. The Bus to Minnesota

Is Harris here?
I'm staring at the fuzz of her hair.
She's looking over my head, and smoking.
She never sees me when she sees me, never has.
He just got the bus, she says.
Will he be back some time later?
I guess he'll call you from Minnesota.

His cousin asked him over.
I nod my head.
He never told me, I'm thinking.
See you, kid, she says,
As she closes the door, firmly.

There's a cloud in the shape of a kangaroo
Just over my head.

Coda

Unforesaken

It's a far cry from me to you,
Across oceans boundless.
Measure the distance with your eye.
It will blind you.

It's a long sob from me to you,
Through streets past knowing,
Where we walked once, arm in arm,
Young, brittle, foolish.

It's a life's span from me to you.
I cannot make it.
If you rise up when you hear this voice,
Count me unforesaken.

About the author

Michael Glover was born in Sheffield. He is currently Poetry Editor of the *Tablet* and a senior art critic and feature writer for the *Independent*. He has been a regular reviewer and commentator upon the world of poetry for the *Economist*, the *New Statesman* and the *Independent*. He has written about poetry in performance for the *Financial Times*. In 2009 he established *The Bow-Wow Shop* (www.bowwowshop.org.uk), a free-to-access, online poetry magazine which has been archived by the British Library.

What other poets and critics have said about Michael Glover's poetry:

'Much energy and brio' – Seamus Heaney, Nobel Prize in Literature, 1995

'Michael Glover's lines unspool gravely and efficiently with few commas – like waves that know they are on their way to someplace, but without making much fuss about it. They can be piercingly sad and hilariously wry, sometimes at the same time. Michael Glover is a major find.' – John Ashbery

'Michael Glover gives us, often dazzlingly, the poet as performer, conjuror, clown, operating with a playfulness which, whether putting forward arguments about language, reality or poetry itself, is artful and frequently highly enjoyable.' – Laurence Sail, *Stand*

'Enviably idiosyncratic and, for that reason, attractive' –Joseph Brodsky, Nobel Prize in Literature, 1987

'Michael Glover, journalist, critic and poet, writes with clarity, wit and, best of all, he makes sense of non-sense.' – Barry Fantoni, co-founder, *Private Eye*

Other poetry publications by Michael Glover:

Measured Lives (1994)
Impossible Horizons (1995)
A Small Modicum of Folly (1997)
The Bead-Eyed Man (1999)
Amidst All This Debris (2001)
For the Sheer Hell of Living (2009)
Only So Much (2011)